From Home to School 2

Stories and Activities for Parents

Ann Gianola

Instructor, San Diego Community College District
San Diego, California

New Readers Press

D0601072

From Home to School Level 2
ISBN 1-56420-304-2
Copyright © 2003 New Readers Press
New Readers Press
Division of ProLiteracy Worldwide
1320 Jamesville Avenue, Syracuse, New York 13210

All rights reserved. No part of this book may be reproduced or transmitted in any form or
by any means, electronic or mechanical, including photocopying, recording, or by any
information storage and retrieval system, without permission in writing from the publisher.

Printed in the United States of America
9 8 7 6 5 4 3

All proceeds from the sale of New Readers Press materials
support literacy programs in the United States and worldwide.

Acquisitions Editor: Paula Schlusberg
Series Editor: Terrie Lipke
Copy Editor: Judi Lauber
Production Director: Heather Witt
Designer: Kimbrly Koennecke
Illustrations: James P. Wallace
Production Specialist: Alexander Jones
Cover Design: Shelagh Clancy

Contents

1. Is your child ever late for school?

2. What does your child do before school?

He Can't Be Late

Alain is late for school almost every day. In the morning, Alain doesn't look at the time. He slowly eats a bowl of cereal. Then he sits in front of the TV watching cartoons. Alain likes cartoons very much. He forgets to turn off the TV and go to school.

Alain's mother looks at the time. She tells Alain to leave, but he doesn't hear her. When the cartoons are over, he turns off the TV. Alain gets up and walks to school. He arrives in class about 15 minutes late, and the teacher is not happy. She marks him tardy again.

Mr. Wilson, the principal, calls Alain's mother. "Your son is often late," says Mr. Wilson. "This is very serious."

"Yes, I know," says Alain's mother. "But he is just a little late. And Alain is only 11 years old."

Mr. Wilson tells Alain's mother that the first few minutes of class are very important. The teacher explains many things, and it is disruptive when Alain is late. His teacher needs to repeat everything for him. "Alain needs to be on time now and when he is an adult," says Mr. Wilson. "He can't be late for work or he will lose his job."

"You're right," says Alain's mother. "He should learn to be on time. It won't happen again."

Answer the Questions

1. How often is Alain late for school?

2. What does Alain eat in the morning?

3. What does Alain watch on TV?

4. What does Alain forget to do?

5. How does Alain get to school?

6. How many minutes late is Alain?

7. What does the teacher do?

8. What does Mr. Wilson say to Alain's mother?

Check the Sentence That Means the Same

1. Alain is late for school almost every day.

   _✔_ **a.** Alain is often late for school.

   ____ **b.** Alain is never late for school.

2. When the cartoons are over, he turns off the TV.

   ____ **a.** He turns off the TV before the cartoons end.

   ____ **b.** He turns off the TV after the cartoons end.

3. He arrives in class about 15 minutes late.

   ____ **a.** He is tardy.

   ____ **b.** He is early.

4. This is very serious.

   ____ **a.** This is a big problem.

   ____ **b.** This is a small problem.

5. It's disruptive when Alain is late.

   ____ **a.** Alain interrupts the class.

   ____ **b.** Alain doesn't interrupt the class.

6. His teacher needs to repeat everything for him.

   ____ **a.** His teacher has to explain things once.

   ____ **b.** His teacher has to explain things again.

Make a List

Some children lose track of time before school. What can cause children to lose track of time?

1. _They watch TV._____.

2. _____.

3. _____.

4. _____.

5. _____.

6. _____.

You're Often Late

Practice the dialog with a partner.

The principal tells me that you're often late for school.

Not very late, Mom. It's only a few minutes.

Late is late. It's disruptive. The teacher needs to repeat directions after you arrive.

Well, I'm just a kid.

It's important for kids and adults to be on time.

OK, Mom. It won't happen again.

Late for School

Listen to the message a parent left on the school answering machine.

> Hello. This is Lori Stoddard. My son, Joey Stoddard, will be late today. Joey has a toothache and needs to see the dentist this morning. Our appointment is at eight-thirty. Hopefully he will get to school by ten o'clock or so. Joey is a fourth-grade student in Miss Benjamin's class. Thank you.

Write the answers.

1. Why will Joey be late for school? <u>He has a dentist appointment.</u>

2. What time is Joey's appointment? _____

3. Why is Joey going to the dentist? _____

4. What time will Joey get to school? _____

5. What grade is Joey in? _____

6. Is this an acceptable reason for being late for school?

   _____

7. What is another acceptable reason for being late for school?

   _____

Answer the Questions

1. Does your child eat slowly in the morning?

2. Does your child watch the time? Do you?

3. Does your child watch TV in the morning?

4. What is your child's favorite TV show?

5. Do you have to remind your child to leave for school? Does your child remember when to leave?

6. Does your child always pay attention to you?

7. What time does your child's school start?

8. Does someone call you if your child is late for school?

9. What is the name of your child's school principal?

10. A principal sometimes needs to talk to a parent. What are some reasons?

Topics for Discussion or Writing

1. Do you think that being a little late for school is serious? Why or why not?

2. Does your child sometimes forget about the time in the morning? What can you do to help your child be on time?

3. What does your child's class do first in the morning? Is this important? Why or why not?

1. What does a school nurse do?

2. What do you know about head lice?

My Head Itches

Ben is sitting at his desk in his third-grade classroom. The other students are doing math. But Ben isn't doing math. He is scratching his head. The teacher walks over to Ben. "What's the matter?" she asks. "Why aren't you working?"

"I can't think," answers Ben. "My head itches, and I can't stop scratching it."

The teacher tells Ben to go to Mrs. Colwell's office. Mrs. Colwell is the school nurse. She looks in Ben's hair. She sees some lice and a few nits. Nits are lice eggs. Mrs. Colwell says, "I found your problem, Ben. You have head lice."

Mrs. Colwell calls Ben's mother. She says Ben needs to go home immediately. He needs to use special shampoo to kill the lice and a fine-tooth comb to remove the nits. He has to stay home until  the lice and nits are all gone. Then he can come back to school.

Later Mrs. Colwell goes to Ben's classroom. She looks in the hair of all the children. She looks for head lice. It's easy to pass head lice from person to person. Mrs. Colwell says, "Don't share hairbrushes and hats with other people."

Mrs. Colwell sends a letter to the parents of the children in Ben's class. She says to contact the school if a child gets head lice. She also says not to worry. Head lice are unpleasant, but they're a common problem.

Answer the Questions

1. Where is Ben sitting?

2. What grade is Ben in?

3. What are the other students doing?

4. Why can't Ben think?

5. Where does the teacher tell Ben to go?

6. What does the school nurse see in Ben's hair?

7. Who does Mrs. Colwell call?

8. When can Ben come back to school?

Complete the Story

completely	immediately	lice	nurse	scratching
hair	itches	nits	✔other	shampoo

Sarah is sitting at her desk in her second-grade classroom. The

_____other_____ students are doing handwriting. But Sarah isn't
          1

doing handwriting. She is _____ her head. Sarah raises
                                    2

her hand and says, "My head _____, and I can't stop
                                        3

scratching it."

The teacher tells Sarah to go to the school _____. The
                                                    4

nurse looks in Sarah's _____. The nurse says, "I found your
                              5

problem. You have head _____."
                              6

The nurse calls Sarah's mother. Sarah needs to go home

_____. The nurse tells Sarah's mother how to get rid of the
        7

lice. She needs to use special _____. She also needs a
                                        8

fine-tooth comb to remove all the _____. Sarah can come
                                          9

back to school when the lice and nits are _____ gone.
                                                  10

What Happened First?

Put these events in order.

____ The nurse examines the hair of the other children.

____ The nurse looks in Ben's hair.

____ The teacher asks, "What's the matter?"

____ Ben says his head itches.

____ The nurse sends a letter to the parents.

_1_ Ben isn't doing math.

____ The teacher tells Ben to go to the nurse's office.

Finding Head Lice

Practice the dialog with a partner.

What's the matter?

My head itches. I can't stop scratching it.

Let me take a look. Ah, I see your problem.

What is it?

You have head lice.

Oh, no! What can we do?

Don't worry. We can take care of it with some special shampoo.

Can I go to school?

No. You need to stay home so other children don't get lice too.

A Letter to Parents

Read this letter from the school nurse.

Shady Tree Elementary

Dear Parents,

Some cases of head lice (pediculosis) have appeared at school. Anyone can get head lice. They are spread from person to person through contact in the classroom and on the playground. Head lice are also passed when children share brushes, combs, hats, and coats. Please contact the school if your child has head lice so that we can check all of the children in the class.

The first sign of head lice is itching. You may also find tiny white eggs (nits) in your child's hair. PLEASE DO NOT SEND YOUR CHILD TO SCHOOL WITH HEAD LICE! Head lice and nits can be easily treated with special shampoos, combs, and cleaning at home. Then bring your child to the nurse's office to be checked before returning to class. And please don't worry. Head lice are unpleasant, but they're a common problem.

Answer the questions.

1. What is another name for head lice?

2. How are head lice spread?

3. Who do you contact if your child has head lice?

4. What is the first sign of head lice?

5. What are nits?

6. How are head lice and nits treated?

7. Why do children with head lice stay home from school?

8. Who does your child have to see before returning to class?

9. Do many children get head lice?

Problem Solving

Your child has head lice. You use the special shampoo. You also use a fine-tooth comb to remove the nits, but it's hard to get all of them. What can you do? Put a check next to the good ideas. Write other good ideas below.

_____ 1. I can send my child to school with a few nits left.

_____ 2. I can repeat the treatment.

_____ 3. I can wash and comb until the nits are all gone.

_____ 4. I can cut my child's hair very short.

_____ 5. I can tell my child not to tell anyone at school.

_____ 6. I can ignore the problem. Head lice aren't serious.

_____ 7. I can call a doctor or nurse for advice.

_✔_ 8. I can _____.

_✔_ 9. I can _____.

Topics for Discussion or Writing

1. What health warnings do you get from your child's school? Which ones are most serious?

2. Do you know another way to treat head lice?

3. What can you do to keep head lice from spreading to other members of your family?

1. Are some students in your child's class from other countries?
2. How can children make friends at school?

She Wants to Be Friends

Naja is a fifth-grade student. She is the only student from Somalia, a country in East Africa. Her native language is Arabic, but Naja is fluent in English.

Every day Naja wears a long skirt, sandals, and a scarf wrapped around her head and neck. Her clothes are very different from the pants and dresses the other girls wear.

Naja is a good student, but she doesn't have any friends in the class. She is very quiet. At lunchtime, she doesn't sit next to anyone. She eats alone. Naja opens a container and eats some vegetables and rice. She looks down at her food. She doesn't make eye contact with the other children.

Jade and Tam are two girls in Naja's class. They sit next to each other at lunch. Today they are eating their sandwiches and talking. Jade says, "I don't like Naja. She isn't very nice. She never talks to anyone."

"I like her," says Tam. "She probably doesn't talk because she is shy. But I think she is nice." Tam feels sorry that Naja is sitting alone. She wants to be friends with her. Then Tam has an idea. She walks over to Naja and says, "Come and sit with us, Naja. And after lunch we can play a game."

Answer the Questions

1. Where is Naja from?

2. What is Naja's native language?

3. Can Naja speak English?

4. What does Naja wear to school?

5. What do the other girls wear to school?

6. Does Naja have friends in the class?

7. Who does Naja sit next to at lunchtime?

8. Who are Jade and Tam?

9. Does Jade like Naja?

10. How does Tam feel when Naja is sitting alone?

Which Category Is It?

China   Mexico   sandwiches   Somalia
dress   pants   scarf   United States
✔fruit   rice   skirt   vegetables

	Lunch Foods		Clothing		Countries
1.	fruit	1.	_____	1.	_____
2.	_____	2.	_____	2.	_____
3.	_____	3.	_____	3.	_____
4.	_____	4.	_____	4.	_____

Same Meaning

Copy the sentence from the story that has the same meaning.

1. She has lunch by herself.

_____.

2. Her first language is Arabic.

_____.

3. Naja can speak English very well.

_____.

Make a List

Write some things the other children notice about Naja.
What does Naja probably notice about the other children?

The children notice	Naja probably notices
1. _____	1. _____
2. _____	2. _____
3. _____	3. _____
4. _____	4. _____
5. _____	5. _____

Questions and Answers

Here are some questions that Tam asks Naja. Write more
questions for Tam. Write answers for Naja. Then practice
asking and answering questions with a partner.

Tam

Naja

1. Are you finished eating?   _No, I am not done yet._ .

2. Do you want to sit with us?   _____ .

3. Do you want to play a game?   _____ .

4. _____ ?   _____ .

5. _____ ?   _____ .

Check the Clothes

What do children wear at your child's school? Put a check next to the clothing they wear. Write other school clothes below.

____ pants   ____ dress   ____ skirt

____ shirt   ____ jeans   ____ sandals

____ shoes   ____ shorts   ____ T-shirt

____ sweater   ____ blouse   ____ sweatshirt

_____   _____   _____

What Are These Children Wearing?

1.    **2.**    **3.**    **4.**

1. _____

2. _____

3. _____

4. _____

Problem Solving

Your child is very shy and doesn't have any friends at school. What can you do? Put a check next to the good ideas. Write other ideas below.

____ **1.** I can tell my child to play with the other children.

____ **2.** I can get angry with my child for not being nice.

____ **3.** I can tell my child that friends are not important.

____ **4.** I can invite some children to play with my child at home.

____ **5.** I can tell my child to be friendlier.

____ **6.** I can find out why the children don't like my child.

____ **7.** I can let my child solve this problem alone.

✔ **8.** I can _____.

✔ **9.** I can _____.

Topics for Discussion or Writing

1. How does a shy child act? Give some examples of what a shy child does at school.

2. Do any children at your child's school wear unusual clothes? Describe what they wear.

3. What are some games that children play at recess? What was your favorite game when you were in school?

1. What does your child eat for lunch at school?
2. What food does the school cafeteria serve?

Don't Throw Away Your Food

Mr. Tran is standing in the cafeteria at West Hills Elementary School. It is 12:00, and he is watching the students during lunchtime. Mr. Tran reminds the children to follow the rules in the cafeteria. He says, "No running! No pushing! And no taking cuts in line!"

The children like Mr. Tran and they listen to him. But sometimes Mr. Tran feels very sad at lunchtime. The children throw away a lot of food. Every day four garbage cans are full. Mr. Tran looks inside and sees sandwiches, apples, bananas, containers full of milk, and many other things.

The children get a lot of food, but eat very little. "Why do you throw away your food?" asks Mr. Tran. Some children say they aren't very hungry. Others say they don't like the food in the cafeteria.

In Vietnam, Mr. Tran's native country, a lot of people were hungry. Many adults and children didn't have enough food to eat. Mr. Tran remembers his life in Vietnam. He was often hungry.

Throwing away food is a big problem at West Hills Elementary School. Mr. Tran wants to talk to the parents and teachers and find an answer. He doesn't want to see good food in garbage cans anymore.

Answer the Questions

1. Where is Mr. Tran standing?

2. What time is it?

3. How does Mr. Tran sometimes feel during lunchtime?

4. How many garbage cans are full every day?

5. Why do the children throw away their food?

6. What is Mr. Tran's native country?

7. Did everyone in Vietnam have enough food to eat?

8. What doesn't Mr. Tran want to see anymore?

Complete the Story

container	friends	pocket	rules	throw
down	garbage	push	sandwich	wait

Cora is standing in line at the school cafeteria. Cora follows all the

_____. She doesn't run. She doesn't _____
         1   2

anyone. Cora gets her tray and sits _____.
                                            3

Cora has a sandwich, an apple, a _____ of milk, and
                                        4

some cookies. She takes a bite of her _____. Then Cora's
                                              5

friend Alana says, "Let's go, Cora. I want to jump rope with you."

"OK," says Cora. She puts the cookies in her _____,
                                                    6

picks up her tray, and walks toward the _____ can.
                                                7

"Just a minute," Mr. Tran says. "What are you doing?"

"I'm going out to play with my _____."
                                      8

"Please sit down and eat your lunch," says Mr. Tran. "Your friends

can _____. You need to eat, and it isn't good to
         9

_____ away food. Please go back to your seat."
     10

Write Some Reasons

Why do some children throw away their food? What can they do instead?

1. <u>The cafeteria food doesn't look good.</u>

 <u>They can bring food they like from home.</u>

2. _____

 _____

Planning for Lunch

Practice the dialog with a partner.

What's for lunch at school today?

The menu says spaghetti on Thursday.

Yuck. I don't like the spaghetti in the cafeteria.

Do you want me to pack you a lunch today?

Yes, please. Can I have a sandwich and some fruit?

Sure. I'll put them in a bag.

May I have cookies too?

Sorry, but we don't have any cookies.

What's for Lunch?

Read this week's school lunch menu.

Lunch Menu — Shady Tree Schools *April*

Monday	Tuesday	Wednesday	Thursday	Friday
2 hamburger, french fries, applesauce, juice, milk	**3** macaroni and cheese, fruit salad, juice, milk	**4** beef tacos, rice, fruit salad, juice, milk	**5** spaghetti, green salad, pineapple, juice, milk	**6** cheese pizza, green salad, pudding, juice, milk
			12	13

Write the answers.

1. What day can your child have spaghetti? _____

2. What day can your child have applesauce? _____

3. What can your child drink at lunch? _____

4. What is the cafeteria serving on Friday? _____

5. Will macaroni and cheese be served on Monday? _____

6. What days can your child have a green salad this week?

   _____

7. What day can your child have rice? _____

8. What kind of fruit is served on Thursday? _____

Problem Solving

Your child doesn't like to eat the food at school. He or she throws away a lot of food. What can you do? Put a check next to the good ideas. Write other ideas below.

____ **1.** I can make my child's lunch at home.

____ **2.** I can tell my child to eat everything.

____ **3.** I can ask the cafeteria to give the children less food.

____ **4.** I can ask the cafeteria to serve better food.

____ **5.** I can tell my child about hungry people in the world.

____ **6.** I won't worry about it. It isn't a big problem.

✔ **7.** I can _____.

✔ **8.** I can _____.

Topics for Discussion or Writing

1. How much time does your child have for lunch? What else does he or she do at lunchtime?

2. What do you do when your child won't eat the food at home? Do you let your child throw away food?

3. Do any places in your community collect food for hungry people?

1. What are some reasons a child might miss school?
2. Do you ever travel with your family? Where?

A Contract
with the Teacher

Ana's mother is talking to Mr. Kennedy after school. Mr. Kennedy is Ana's third-grade teacher. Ana's mother tells him that she and Ana are going to California. They need to help Ana's grandmother. She is having surgery. Ana will be absent from school for one month.

Mr. Kennedy explains that they all need to sign a contract. That means that Ana promises to do all her schoolwork in California. Her mother can help her and make sure it is finished. Mr. Kennedy will check her schoolwork when she returns. Ana, her mother, and Mr. Kennedy sign the contract.

Ana leaves for California the next week. She brings all her schoolwork. Every morning Ana studies at her grandmother's house. She reads, writes, and does math. Then her mother checks her

work. In the evening, Ana does her science and social studies assignments. Ana's mother checks her work again.

Ana returns from California after one month. Her grandmother is better. Mr. Kennedy and the students are very happy to see her. She gives Mr. Kennedy her schoolwork. It is all finished. "Good job, Ana!" says Mr. Kennedy. "Now tell us about California."

Answer the Questions

1. Who is talking to Mr. Kennedy after school?

2. Where are Ana and her mother going?

3. Who do Ana and her mother need to help?

4. What do Ana, her mother, and Mr. Kennedy need to sign?

5. What does Ana promise to do?

6. Who signs the contract?

7. When does Ana leave for California?

8. What does Ana do in the morning in California?

9. When does Ana return from California?

10. How is Ana's grandmother?

Which Category Is It?

assignment	Florida	New York	Texas
California	lesson	project	week
day	month	report	year

Periods of Time	Schoolwork	States in the U.S.
1. _____	1. _____	1. _____
2. _____	2. _____	2. _____
3. _____	3. _____	3. _____
4. _____	4. _____	4. _____

Matching

Match the sentences that mean the same.

____ 1. She will be absent.

____ 2. She is having surgery.

____ 3. They're happy to see her.

____ 4. They sign the contract.

____ 5. It is all finished.

____ 6. She does a good job.

____ 7. Ana promises to study.

a. They're glad she's back.

b. She is having an operation.

c. She does nice work.

d. It is completed.

e. Ana says she will study.

f. She will not be in school.

g. They write their names on an agreement.

What Happened First?

Put these events in order.

____ Ana returns from California after one month.

____ Ana leaves for California the next week.

____ Mr. Kennedy explains about the contract.

_1_ Ana's mother tells the teacher that they are going to California for one month.

____ Mr. Kennedy and the students are very happy to see Ana.

____ Every morning Ana studies at her grandmother's house.

____ Ana, her mother, and Mr. Kennedy sign the contract.

Looking at Schoolwork

Practice the dialog with a partner.

What's your assignment for today?

I need to read Chapter 3 in my book. Then I have a couple of pages of math.

Tell me when you're finished. Then I can look at your answers.

Do I have to do it right now?

Yes, please do it now. You can take a break when you're done.

Can I watch TV when I'm done?

Yes. If your answers are correct, you can watch TV.

Ana's Book Report

Look at Ana's book report worksheet.

Report on My Favorite Book

1. Title: __Albert in the Amazon__
2. Author: _____
3. Illustrator: __Pearl Jameson__
4. What type of book is it? __It's an adventure story.__
5. Who are the characters? __The characters are Albert, Sancho, a big snake, and others.__
6. What is the setting? __This story takes place in the jungle, but some parts are in a city.__
7. What is the most exciting part of the story? __Albert meets Sancho and they explore the jungle. Sometimes they have problems and almost get hurt. But most of the time they have fun.__

Answer the questions.

1. Which item does Ana forget to answer?

2. How does Ana describe the type of book?

3. Are there pictures in this book? How do you know?

4. Are there some characters in the book that Ana doesn't name? How do you know?

5. What more can Ana write to describe the setting?

6. Do you think Ana writes a good answer to question 7? Can you think of any way she can make it better?

7. Does Ana like this book? How do you know?

Answer the Questions

1. What is the name of your child's teacher?

2. What grade is your child in?

3. Where do your relatives live?

4. Do you ever visit relatives during the school year?

5. Does your child ever miss school for reasons other than illness?

6. Do you ever sign contracts with your child's teacher?

7. Do you ever correct your child's schoolwork?

8. What subjects are easy for you to correct?

9. What subjects are difficult for you to correct?

10. Do you make sure your child's schoolwork is finished?

Topics for Discussion or Writing

1. Would you ever take your child out of school for a long time? Why or why not?

2. Is one month a long time to miss school? What things will a child miss when he or she is absent for a month?

3. If you have a family emergency, can you help your child with schoolwork at the same time? Why or why not?

1. What do you know about field trips?
2. Why do parent volunteers go along on field trips?

The Field Trip

Mr. Dugan is going on a field trip to the zoo. He is a parent volunteer for his son's class. Mr. Dugan and the other parent volunteers get on the bus with the children. The bus is noisy. The children are very excited.

Everyone gets off the bus at the zoo. Mr. Dugan is watching four children. He has Alex, Buan, Jake, and his son, Michael. The teacher tells the children to stay with their group.

Mr. Dugan's group enters the zoo. First they see the elephants. The elephants are walking around. Next they see the bears. The bears are playing in the sun. Then they go and see the lions. The lions are sleeping.

"Michael," Mr. Dugan says. "Look at the lions!"

"Where's Jake?" asks Buan.

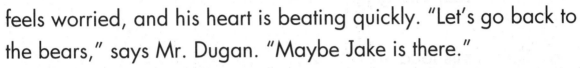

Mr. Dugan turns around and sees Alex, Buan, and Michael. But he doesn't see Jake. Mr. Dugan feels worried, and his heart is beating quickly. "Let's go back to the bears," says Mr. Dugan. "Maybe Jake is there."

Mr. Dugan and the children return to the bears. There is Jake. He is looking at the bears. "Jake! Here you are," says Mr. Dugan. "You need to stay with the group!"

"The lions are sleeping. That is boring," says Jake. "The bears are playing. That is more interesting."

"Boring or interesting, we need to stay together," says Mr. Dugan. "I don't want to lose you at the zoo."

Answer the Questions

1. Where is Mr. Dugan going?

2. How is everyone getting to the zoo?

3. How many children is Mr. Dugan watching?

4. What does the teacher tell the children to do?

5. What animals do they see first?

6. What are the lions doing?

7. How does Mr. Dugan feel when he doesn't see Jake?

8. Why did Jake return to the bears?

Check the Sentence That Means the Same

1. He is a parent volunteer for his son's class.

_____ **a.** He helps when his son's class needs him.

_____ **b.** He is in his son's class.

2. The bus is noisy.

_____ **a.** The bus is loud.

_____ **b.** The bus is quiet.

3. The teacher tells the children to stay with their group.

_____ **a.** The teacher tells the children to look at interesting things.

_____ **b.** The teacher tells the children to stay together.

4. The lions are sleeping.

_____ **a.** The lions are resting.

_____ **b.** The lions are eating.

5. The bears are more interesting.

_____ **a.** The bears are more fun to watch.

_____ **b.** The bears are boring to watch.

6. Mr. Dugan and the children return to the bears.

_____ **a.** Mr. Dugan and the children don't look at the bears.

_____ **b.** Mr. Dugan and the children go back to see
the bears again.

What Happened First?

Put these events in order.

____   The lions are sleeping.

____   Jake is looking at the bears.

_1_   Mr. Dugan and the other volunteers get on the bus.

____   Mr. Dugan's group enters the zoo.

____   Mr. Dugan says, "We need to stay together."

____   First they see the elephants.

____   Buan asks, "Where's Jake?"

Reporting a Lost Child

Practice the dialog with a partner.

I'm looking for a lost boy. His name is Devon.

Can you describe him?

He's about six years old. He has dark brown hair.

What is he wearing?

He's wearing a red T-shirt and blue pants.

Where did you last see him?

He was right here by the gate, just a few minutes ago.

Don't worry. We'll help you find him.

Class Field Trip

Read this letter about a class field trip.

Field Trip Permission Form — Shady Tree Elementary

Our class is taking a field trip to the San Francisco Zoo on Wednesday, April 5. A bus will leave school at 9:00 A.M. and return from the zoo at 1:30 P.M. Please make sure that your child brings a sack lunch from home. Drinks will be provided at the zoo.

Please have your child wear comfortable walking shoes, a hat, and sunscreen. A fee of $2.50 is needed to cover the cost of the bus transportation. Please send it along with the permission slip below.

We will need 5 parent volunteers to accompany us. To volunteer, please contact Mrs. Patterson through the school office at 555-9871.

****

I, _____ (Parent's name) give permission for my child,

_____ (Child's name) to attend the field trip to the San Francisco Zoo on Wednesday April 5.

_____ (Parent's signature) _____ (Date)

Answer the questions.

1. Can a child who arrives at school at 9:15 on Wednesday go on the field trip?

2. How much is the fee? What is it for?

3. What does your child need to bring from home?

4. What does your child need to wear?

5. How many parent volunteers are needed?

6. What do you think the parent volunteers will do?

7. Which part of this letter do you return?

8. What does it mean to give permission?

Answer the Questions

1. How often does your child go on field trips?

2. What places do schoolchildren go on field trips?

3. What is the name of the nearest zoo?

4. Have you ever gone to the zoo with your child? If yes, what did you see?

5. Do you ever volunteer to go on field trips?

6. Why is it easier to watch a small group of children than a large group?

7. Has your child ever gotten lost?

8. How does someone feel when a child gets lost?

9. Why do some children wander away from a group?

10. Where are some places that children can get lost?

Topics for Discussion or Writing

1. What can you do so that your child doesn't get lost? Have you talked to your child about what to do if he or she can't find you?

2. What would you do if your child was lost?

3. How can parent volunteers help in class? Have you ever volunteered?

1. How often do you get your child's report card?
2. What subjects are graded on your child's report card?

The Report Card

Roza walks outside and unlocks her mailbox. She picks up the telephone bill, some ads, and a letter from North Bay Elementary School. Roza's daughter, Sonya, is a student there. Roza opens the envelope. It is Sonya's report card.

Sonya gets three report cards a year. The report card shows how Sonya is doing in school. Roza doesn't read English very well. Roza can read some of the letters and numbers on the report card, but she doesn't understand what they mean.

There are also a lot of comments from Sonya's teacher. Roza can't understand the teacher's comments.

She needs a dictionary. Is this a good report card or not? What does everything mean? Roza understood Sonya's last two report cards. She got them at a conference with the teacher. A translator was there to explain everything. But today there is no translator. Roza is alone.

Roza thinks about asking a neighbor to read Sonya's report card. But she doesn't want a neighbor to know what the teacher says about her daughter. A report card is personal. She can ask Sonya to read the report card. But what if Sonya doesn't tell her everything? Roza holds the report card in her hand. She doesn't know what to do.

Answer the Questions

1. What is in Roza's mailbox?

2. How many report cards does Sonya get a year?

3. What does the report card show?

4. Does Roza understand what the letters and numbers mean?

5. Where did Roza get the last two report cards?

6. Who was there to explain everything?

7. Why doesn't Roza want to ask a neighbor to read Sonya's report card?

8. Does Roza want Sonya to read the report card to her?

Complete the Story

another	explain	letters	report	translator
daughter	know	questions	school	writes

Today Roza is going to North Bay Elementary School. She is there

to talk to the teacher and get her daughter's _____ card.
                                                       1

Roza shakes hands with the teacher, Miss Baxter. She also meets

_____ person. His name is Mr. Sergeev, and he is the
        2

_____. He is there to help Roza understand the report
        3

card. He can help her ask any _____.
                                        4

The report card tells how Roza's daughter is doing in

_____. Roza doesn't read English very well. She can read
        5

some of the _____ and numbers on this report card, but
                      6

she doesn't understand what they mean. Mr. Sergeev is there to

_____ everything to her.
        7

The teacher _____ comments on the report card about
                        8

Roza's _____. Mr. Sergeev helps Roza and Miss Baxter
              9

communicate. They are happy to have him. They wouldn't

_____ what to do without a translator.
        10

Make a List

What questions can a parent ask a teacher about a child's report card? What can the teacher ask a parent?

1. A parent can ask, "How is my child doing in reading?"

2. _____

3. _____

4. A teacher can ask, _____

5. _____

6. _____

Talking about a Report Card

Practice the dialog with a partner.

What's wrong? You look confused.

I don't understand something about this report card.

What is it? Maybe I can help you.

It's a letter for a citizenship grade. It says G.

The G means "Good."

OK. What does the number 3 mean over here?

Let's look at the report card and see if the number is explained.

Sonya's Report Card

Read these comments from the teacher on Sonya's report card.

Teacher Comments: Sonya is making great progress this year in reading and writing. She is an organized student and finishes her work on time. She also enjoys writing stories and then reading them aloud.

Math is sometimes a problem for Sonya. She needs to slow down and work more carefully. In class, I encourage her to check her work before she hands it in. Please continue to practice math with her at home. It will help a lot.

I enjoy having Sonya in our class. She is a very good citizen and is well liked by the other children.

Answer the questions.

1. In what areas is Sonya making great progress?

2. Is Sonya often late completing her work?

3. What does Sonya enjoy doing?

4. What is sometimes a problem for Sonya?

5. What does Sonya's teacher do in class?

6. What does the teacher ask Sonya's parents to continue at home?

7. Do the other children like Sonya?

8. How do you think Sonya's parents feel after reading these comments?

Answer the Questions

1. Is your child's report card hand delivered or mailed?

2. When does your child get a report card?

3. What is the first thing you look for on a report card?

4. Is the report card difficult or easy to understand?

5. What kind of questions do you have about a report card?

6. Does your child's school offer translators if necessary?

7. Do you discuss the report card with your child? With the teacher?

8. What do you do if your child has a good report card?

9. What do you do if your child doesn't have a good report card?

10. Do you ever show your child's report card to other people?

Topics for Discussion or Writing

1. Describe the report card your child's school uses. What do the letters, numbers, or check marks mean?

2. What part of your child's report card is the most important to you? Why?

3. Do you always agree with everything a teacher writes on a report card? Why or why not?

1. What are some places that have after-school programs?
2. What activities do after-school programs offer?

After-School Care

School is over at 2:45 P.M. The bell rings and the children leave their classrooms. Some children walk home. Some children get on buses because they don't live near the school. Sovann and other children stay at school because they go to after-school care.

Sovann usually stays at school until about 5:30 P.M. Sovann's father and mother work. They don't want Sovann to be home alone in the afternoon. Many children from Sovann's class and other classes go to after-school care.

After-school care is different from school. Adults are there to help, but children can play outside. Sovann likes to go out on the playground after school. He likes to play ball with his friend Eli.

When he gets tired, he goes inside. He sits at a table and does his homework. He doesn't want to have too much homework to finish at home.

At 5:30, Sovann's father picks him up. Sovann and his father are happy to see each other. Sovann is ready to go home. He is hungry for dinner. It's been a long day.

Answer the Questions

1. What time is school over?

2. What happens when the bell rings?

3. How do the children get home?

4. What does Sovann do?

5. How late does Sovann usually stay at school?

6. Why don't Sovann's parents want him to go home after school?

7. Is after-school care the same as school?

8. Who does Sovann like to play ball with?

9. Why does Sovann do his homework at after-school care?

10. How does Sovann get home?

Check the Sentence That Means the Same

1. School is over at 2:45 P.M.

    ____ **a.** Classes begin at 2:45 P.M.

    ____ **b.** Classes end at 2:45 P.M.

2. Sovann's father and mother work.

    ____ **a.** Sovann's parents have jobs.

    ____ **b.** Sovann's parents don't have jobs.

3. They don't want Sovann to be home alone in the afternoon.

    ____ **a.** They don't want Sovann to be by himself.

    ____ **b.** They don't want Sovann to have friends in the house.

4. He doesn't want to have too much homework to do at home.

    ____ **a.** He likes doing homework at home.

    ____ **b.** He doesn't like doing homework at home.

5. At 5:30, Sovann's father picks him up.

    ____ **a.** Sovann's father drops him off at 5:30.

    ____ **b.** Sovann's father comes to get him at 5:30.

6. It's been a long day.

    ____ **a.** It feels like a lot of time has passed.

    ____ **b.** It feels like a little time has passed.

Write Some Reasons

Why do some parents think an after-school program is a
good idea? Why do some children think after-school care is
a good idea?

1. *Some parents think* _____

2. _____

3. _____

4. *Some children think* _____

5. _____

6. _____

Staying Late

Practice the dialog with a partner.

Hello. How can I help you?

I need to pick up my son a little late today.

What time will you be here?

**Probably about five forty-five instead of five
thirty. I need to work late.**

Please remember that we close at six o'clock.

**I understand. Oh, please tell my son that I'll
be there soon.**

No problem. He's right here. I'll tell him.

After-School Program Rules

Read this information for parents about the after-school care program.

Shady Tree Elementary
After-School Program Rules

The after-school care program is open Monday through Friday from 3:00 to 6:00 P.M.
All children need to be picked up by 6:00 P.M.

- There are no exceptions. If a child is not picked up, then emergency contacts will be called.
- Parents who are late may be charged a late fee.
- If parents are often late, their child may be withdrawn from the program.
- The after-school program is closed on holidays and during winter break.

Write the answers.

1. What time does the after-school program begin? _____

2. By what time do children need to be picked up? _____

3. Who is called if a child is not picked up? _____

4. What can happen if parents are often late? _____

5. Is the after-school program open on Memorial Day? _____

6. How many hours can a child spend in after-school care in one week? _____

7. Can children go to after-school care during winter break?

_____

Problem Solving

Your 8-year-old child gets out of school at 2:30. You don't get home from work until 4:00. What can you do? Put a check next to the good ideas. Write other good ideas below.

_____ **1.** I can enroll my child in an after-school program.

_____ **2.** I can let my child stay home alone for a while.

_____ **3.** I can find a babysitter.

_____ **4.** I can have my child visit a friend after school.

_____ **5.** I can tell my child to wait for me near the school.

_____ **6.** I can tell my child to help the teacher after school.

_____ **7.** I can ask another parent to pick up my child.

✓ **8.** I can _____.

✓ **9.** I can _____.

Topics for Discussion or Writing

1. At what age do you think it is safe for a child to be home alone after school?

2. Why do parents worry about a child who is home alone? What can happen if a child is left alone?

1. What are some things that can hurt a child's feelings?
2. How can you tell when your child is upset?

Hurt Feelings at School

Inés returns home from school and puts down her backpack. She doesn't say hello to anyone. She doesn't go to the kitchen for a snack. She walks straight to her bedroom and closes the door.

Inés's father hears her crying. He knocks on her door and then opens it. Inés is sitting on the floor. She is crying. Her father puts his hand on her shoulder. He asks, "Inés, why are you crying?"

Inés explains that two girls at school are teasing her. They make fun of her clothes. They call her bad names. Inés says, "They tell me I am stupid and ugly."

Inés says that she does not make fun of them. She does not call them bad names. Inés says, "Those girls hurt my feelings every day! I don't want to go to school anymore. They are making my life miserable."

Inés's father feels furious. He wants to call the principal immediately. He says the girls are breaking a school rule. The rule says you must treat other people with respect. He says, "You are not stupid or ugly. You don't have to listen to that. Who are these girls? What are their names?"

Inés says, "No, Dad. Then it will be worse. Just forget about it."

Answer the Questions

1. Where does Inés go when she returns home from school?

2. What does Inés's father hear?

3. What does Inés's father do?

4. How many girls are teasing Inés?

5. What do the girls make fun of?

6. What do the girls call her?

7. What are they doing to Inés's life?

8. Who does Inés's father want to call immediately?

9. What rule are the girls breaking?

10. Does Inés tell her father the girls' names?

Which Category Is It?

angry	depressed	furious	notebook
backpack	door	lunchbox	pencils
ceiling	floor	miserable	window

School Supplies	Emotions	Parts of a Room
1. _____	1. _____	1. _____
2. _____	2. _____	2. _____
3. _____	3. _____	3. _____
4. _____	4. _____	4. _____

Matching

Match the parts of the sentences.

____ 1. She does not call   a. to go to school anymore.

____ 2. Inés's father hears   b. her life miserable.

____ 3. The girls are breaking   c. on the floor.

____ 4. She doesn't want   d. them bad names.

____ 5. They are making   e. her bedroom.

____ 6. She walks straight to   f. her crying.

____ 7. Inés is sitting   g. a school rule.

What Happened First?

Put these events in order.

_____ Her father hears Inés crying.

_____ Inés says, "I don't want to go to school anymore."

__1__ Inés returns home from school and puts down her backpack.

_____ Inés's father wants to call the principal immediately.

_____ Inés says, "Just forget about it."

_____ Inés walks straight to her bedroom and closes the door.

_____ Inés explains that two girls at school are teasing her.

Reporting a Problem

Practice the dialog with a partner.

This is the principal speaking. What can I do for you?

I'm calling to report a problem at school.

What kind of problem?

Two girls at school are harassing my daughter.

That is a problem. Harassment is against school rules.

My daughter is very upset. They're making her life miserable.

Thanks for reporting this. Now please give me more information about what's happening.

Check the Behaviors

What are some mean things children do and say? Put a check next to things schoolchildren do to be mean. Write other mean actions below.

____ call someone names

____ hit someone

____ help someone up

____ push someone down

____ pull someone's hair

____ steal from someone

____ make fun of someone

____ share with someone

_____   _____

What Is Happening to These Students?

1.   **2.**   **3.**   **4.**

 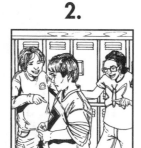  

1. _____

2. _____

3. _____

4. _____

Problem Solving

Two children at school are teasing your child. Your child is upset but doesn't want you to do anything about it. What can you do? Put a check next to the good ideas. Write other good ideas below.

_____ **1.** I can call each child's parents and complain.

_____ **2.** I can ignore the problem. All kids get teased sometimes.

_____ **3.** I can transfer my child to another school.

_____ **4.** I can tell the two children to leave my child alone.

_____ **5.** I can report the problem to the principal.

_____ **6.** I can teach my child to fight back.

_____ **7.** I can call the police.

✓ **8.** I can _____.

✓ **9.** I can _____.

Topics for Discussion or Writing

1. What does your child usually do after school? How do you know when something is bothering your child?

2. Did anyone tease you when you were a child? If yes, what did they tease you about? How did you handle it?

3. In your opinion, is teasing serious enough to report to a teacher or principal? If not, what kind of problem is serious enough?

1. What math skills do children learn in school?
2. Why should children learn multiplication?

He Can't Do Multiplication

Pavel has a difficult homework assignment. He needs to correct all the wrong answers on his multiplication test. How can Pavel correct his test? He doesn't know the answers!

Pavel doesn't like multiplication. He counts on his fingers. He uses a pencil and paper. He can't remember the answers.

"Help me," says Pavel to his father. "I don't get it. What is 4 x 8? Is it 30? Is it 32? I don't remember."

"Pavel," says his father. "You need to memorize the answers to multiplication. I think multiplication is fun!"

Pavel's father goes to the store and buys multiplication flash cards. Every evening Pavel and his father practice with the flash cards. Soon Pavel learns multiplication. He doesn't have to count on his  fingers. He doesn't have to use a paper and pencil. He can remember the answers.

After the next multiplication test, Pavel doesn't have a homework assignment. He doesn't have any wrong answers. All of his answers are right. Now Pavel agrees with his father. Multiplication is fun!

Answer the Questions

1. What is Pavel's homework assignment?

2. Does Pavel like multiplication?

3. How does Pavel do multiplication?

4. Who does Pavel ask for help with his multiplication?

5. What does Pavel's father say that he needs to do?

6. What does Pavel's father buy?

7. How often do Pavel and his father practice with the flash cards?

8. Does Pavel learn multiplication?

9. Why doesn't Pavel have a homework assignment after the next test?

Complete the Story

addition	assignment	fingers	needs	remember
answers	doesn't	flash cards	practice	wrong

Alisha has a difficult homework assignment. She needs to correct
her addition test. She got many _____ answers. How can
1
she do the assignment? She doesn't know the _____.
2

Alisha doesn't like doing _____. She can't
3
_____ the answer for 5 + 4. She can't add in her head.
4
She counts on her _____.
5

Alisha's mother says she _____ to memorize the
6
answers to addition. She buys a package of addition
_____. Every morning Alisha and her mother
7
_____ with the flash cards. Soon Alisha knows the
8
answers quickly. She doesn't have to count on her fingers.

After the next addition test, Alisha doesn't have a homework
_____. She _____ have any wrong answers.
9　　　　　　　　　　10
Addition is fun!

Make a List

Pavel doesn't like multiplication. What other subjects don't children like, and why? What can you do to help?

1. _____

   _____

2. _____

   _____

3. _____

   _____

Practicing Multiplication

Practice the dialog with a partner.

What is 7 x 6?

I can't remember.

Do you remember 6 x 7?

Yes. The answer is 42.

Well, 7 x 6 is the same as 6 x 7.

Oh, I understand. So 7 x 6 is also 42.

That's right!

Ask me another one.

OK. What is 3 x 9?

I know that! It's 27.

Parent-Teacher Conference

Listen to the comments from Alisha's teacher to her parents at conference time.

Every week we have a timed addition test. We give the students five minutes to answer fifty addition problems. Alisha has a very hard time. She is unsure of the answers, feels nervous, and starts guessing. Don't worry. Several of the students are having a difficult time with this. I suggest that you continue to practice basic addition facts with her at home. You can borrow a set of flash cards from the classroom if you like. It's important that Alisha feel confident about solving problems now and in the future. She can do it!

Write the answers.

1. How often do the students have a timed test? _____

2. How many minutes do they have? _____

3. How many questions do they need to answer? _____

4. How does Alisha do? _____

5. What does Alisha do when she does not know the answer?

_____

6. What does the teacher suggest Alisha's parents do?

_____

7. What does the teacher say is important? _____

Problem Solving

Your child doesn't like a subject at school. What can you do? Put a check next to the good ideas. Write other good ideas below.

____ **1.** I can talk to the teacher and get more help.

____ **2.** I can work on the subject with my child at home.

____ **3.** I can find out why my child doesn't like the subject.

____ **4.** I can tell my child that he or she isn't very smart.

____ **5.** I can tell my child that I didn't like the subject either.

____ **6.** I can find ways to make the subject more interesting.

✔ **7.** I can _____.

✔ **8.** I can _____.

Topics for Discussion or Writing

1. Did you have a difficult time with something in school? What did you do to improve?

2. How can you help your child feel more confident about something that is difficult?

3. Is it important to do something about a problem your child has in school? Why or why not?

1. How do some children misbehave at school?
2. When is it OK to talk in class?

She Talks Too Much

Justine is a very popular girl. Justine likes everyone, and everyone likes her. She is also very smart. But Justine has one problem. She's always talking in class. Justine turns to her left and talks to Matt. She turns to her right and talks to Becky.

Miss Campos, the teacher, wants Justine to behave in class. She moves Justine from seat to seat because Justine's always talking. But Justine finds someone to talk to wherever she sits.

One day Miss Campos moves Justine next to Albert. Albert is the quietest boy in the class. He never talks.

But after a few minutes, Justine is talking to Albert. They are good friends now. Albert is busy talking and listening to Justine.

Now Miss Campos is angry. She tells Justine that sometimes it's OK to talk in class. But other times she needs to listen. "When you are talking, you are not listening," says Miss Campos. "I have to repeat things for you. And I don't appreciate that."

Justine says that she is very sorry. She says that she isn't going to talk anymore. Miss Campos says, "Thank you, Justine. I'm going to give you one more chance. But this is it. If you can't be quiet, then you can sit at a table alone."

Answer the Questions

1. What is Justine's problem?

2. What does Miss Campos want Justine to do?

3. Where does Miss Campos tell Justine to sit?

4. Does Albert always talk?

5. What happens after a few minutes?

6. How does Miss Campos feel?

7. What is Justine not doing if she is talking?

8. What does Justine say?

9. What does Miss Campos give Justine?

10. Where can Justine sit if she can't be quiet?

Check the Sentence That Means the Same

1. Justine is a very popular girl.

_____ **a.** Everyone likes Justine.

_____ **b.** Justine likes everyone.

2. The teacher wants Justine to behave in class.

_____ **a.** The teacher wants Justine to be quiet and listen.

_____ **b.** The teacher wants Justine to talk and have a good time.

3. Albert is the quietest boy in the class.

_____ **a.** Albert doesn't make a lot of noise.

_____ **b.** Albert talks a lot.

4. When you are talking, you are not listening.

_____ **a.** You can talk and listen at the same time.

_____ **b.** You can't talk and listen at the same time.

5. She's going to give Justine one more chance.

_____ **a.** She is moving Justine right now.

_____ **b.** She will move Justine if she talks again.

6. If you can't be quiet, then you can sit at a table alone.

_____ **a.** You can sit by yourself if you don't stop talking.

_____ **b.** You can sit with Matt and Becky again.

What Happened First?

Put these events in order.

____ One day Miss Campos moves Justine next to Albert.

____ The teacher moves Justine from seat to seat.

____ Miss Campos is very angry.

__1__ Justine likes everyone, and everyone likes her.

____ After a few minutes, Justine is talking to Albert.

____ Miss Campos gives Justine one more chance.

____ Justine says that she is very sorry.

You Aren't Listening

Practice the dialog with a partner.

Excuse me—are you listening?

Yes, Miss Campos. I'm listening.

OK, what did I just say?

I don't know.

You don't know because you weren't listening. You were talking. Now I need to repeat what I said.

I'm sorry. I'm ready to listen now.

If you don't pay attention in class, I will have to talk to your parents.

A Note from the Teacher

You are Justine's parent. You get this note from her teacher. Read it.

Dear Mr. and Mrs. Cassatt,

Justine did not obey our classroom rule about not talking today. I had to remind her three times to be quiet while the other students were busy listening and working. After that, as you know, I must write a note to inform you of the problem.

Justine is a wonderful girl, and everyone enjoys her company. However, she has a problem of making conversation with other students at inappropriate times. Thank you for your concern.

Sincerely,

Miss Campos

Miss Campos

Write a note back to the teacher. Think about what you will say and how you can help Justine behave better in class.

Dear Miss Campos,

_____

_____

_____

_____

_____

_____

_____

Answer the Questions

1. Does your child talk a lot, or is your child quiet?

2. Who does your child sit next to in class?

3. Is your child allowed to sit next to friends?

4. Does your child's teacher sometimes move seats around?

5. What are the rules about talking in your child's class?

6. What does your child's teacher get angry about?

7. How does your child's teacher discipline a student?

8. What is a polite way to ask a child to stop talking?

9. What is an impolite way to ask a child to stop talking?

10. Have you ever gotten a note from your child's teacher?

11. How do you discipline your child at home?

Topics for Discussion or Writing

1. If you were Justine's teacher, how would you help Justine change her behavior?

2. What is another behavior problem a child can have at school? How can you solve it?

3. Do you think talking a lot in class is a serious problem? Why or why not?

Lesson 12

1. What do children like to do together after school?
2. Do you have rules about your child visiting friends?

Invitation to a Friend's House

John and Shiro are very good friends at school. They get along well. John invites Shiro to come over to his house tomorrow. They can play together after school.

Shiro feels very excited. When he comes home, he tells his father about his invitation to go to John's house. "John is very nice," says Shiro. "He has a big dog and a lot of computer games!"

Shiro's father feels uncomfortable. He doesn't know John. He doesn't know where John lives. Is a parent at John's house to watch the boys? Is John's neighborhood safe? What if the dog bites? Also, Shiro's father doesn't like him to play a lot of computer games.

Shiro's father says, "I don't like this idea. We have a rule about not going to other people's houses." He doesn't want Shiro to go to John's house. He wants his son to come home after school.

Shiro is safe at home. "You can play with John at school," Shiro's father says. "That's enough time together."

Shiro is very upset. "What do I tell John?" he asks.

Shiro's father has this rule for a reason. He doesn't want anything bad to happen to his son. "I'm sorry to disappoint you," Shiro's father says. "I don't want to hurt John's feelings. But you have to tell him that's our rule."

Answer the Questions

1. How do John and Shiro get along?

2. When does John want Shiro to come over?

3. How does Shiro feel when he comes home?

4. What kind of pet does John have?

5. How does Shiro's father feel?

6. Does Shiro's father know John?

7. What does Shiro's father have a rule about?

8. Where does Shiro's father want his son to go after school?

9. Where can Shiro play with John?

10. What is the reason that Shiro's father has this rule?

Which Category Is It?

apartment	dog	house	townhouse
cat	excited	mobile home	turtle
disappointed	fish	sorry	uncomfortable

Places to Live   **Pets**   **Emotions**

1. _____   1. _____   1. _____

2. _____   2. _____   2. _____

3. _____   3. _____   3. _____

4. _____   4. _____   4. _____

Same Meaning

Copy the sentence from the story that has the same meaning.

1. John asks Shiro to come for a visit tomorrow.

_____

2. He does not know what John's address is.

_____

3. I don't want to make John feel bad.

_____

Write Some Reasons

Write some things that your family has rules about.
Explain why each rule is important.

1. <u>I don't let my child visit people that I don't know.</u>

   <u>I worry less if he is with people I already know.</u>

2. _____

   _____

3. _____

   _____

Questions and Answers

Here are some answers that Shiro has for his father. Write
the questions for his father to ask. Write more questions
that a parent might ask, and answer them. Then practice
asking and answering questions with a partner.

Father   **Shiro**

1. <u>What are you going to do?</u>   We're going to play games.

2. _____   He lives in Oak Park.

3. _____   I think his mom is at home.

4. _____   _____

5. _____   _____

A Message from Mrs. Anderson

Listen to the message from John's mother to Shiro's parents on their answering machine.

Hello, Mr. and Mrs. Yoshimura. This is Kathleen Anderson. My son John and your son Shiro are friends at school. I'm calling to invite Shiro to come over and play with John after school tomorrow. If you feel comfortable, Shiro can ride the bus with John to our house. Also, I'm working until about five o'clock. There will be a babysitter here in the afternoon—Lisa. She's great. Anyway, I'll be home after that. And I don't mind driving Shiro home whenever you need him. We would be happy to have him. You can call me at home this evening: 555-7410.
Thanks. Bye.

Write the answers.

1. What is the caller's name? _____

2. Why is she calling? _____

3. How can Shiro get to John's house? _____

4. Where is the mother before 5:00? _____

5. Who is home in the afternoon? _____

6. How can Shiro get home? _____

7. What is Mrs. Anderson's telephone number? _____

8. What do you think Shiro's father will say? Why? _____

_____

Answer the Questions

1. Who are your child's friends at school?

2. Do you know the families of your child's friends?

3. Does your child play with any children outside of school?

4. Do you prefer your child to play with other children in your home or somewhere else?

5. How do you feel about your child playing computer games?

6. Does your child play with friends at school?

7. How many children live in your neighborhood?

8. How often does your child get invited to a friend's house?

9. What rules do you talk about with your child before he or she visits another family?

Topics for Discussion or Writing

1. What concerns do you have about your child visiting another child's home? What do you not allow your child to do?

2. What is a good way to get to know the parents of your child's friends? How do some people help you feel comfortable?

3. How do you say no to an invitation without hurting someone's feelings?

1. What kind of clothes does your child like to wear?
2. Does your child's school have a dress code?

The School Dress Code

Kiara goes to Lincoln Elementary School. Most of the students at Lincoln follow the dress code. The school colors are blue and white. Kiara wears a white blouse and blue pants or a blue skirt to school. She doesn't spend a lot of time looking in her closet every morning. Getting dressed for school is fast and easy.

Students don't have to follow the dress code. It's voluntary. Parents can decide if they want their children to follow the dress code or not. Kiara's parents want her to follow the dress code. They like their daughter to dress like the other children.

One of Kiara's friends never follows the dress code. Her name is Shannon. Shannon's parents don't think a dress code is important. Shannon doesn't wear blue and white clothes. Shannon's clothes are red, yellow, green, purple, and orange! Her clothes look colorful and very stylish.

Kiara wants to dress like Shannon. She doesn't want to follow the dress code. She is tired of blue and white. It's boring to wear the same colors and the same clothes day after day. Kiara wants her parents to say that she doesn't have to follow the dress code. She wants to wear clothes that are colorful and stylish too.

Answer the Questions

1. What is the name of Kiara's school?

2. How do most students at Lincoln dress?

3. What does Kiara wear to school?

4. What do Kiara's parents want her to do?

5. Who never follows the dress code?

6. How do Shannon's clothes look?

7. How does Kiara feel about blue and white?

8. What kind of clothes does Kiara want?

Complete the Story

casual	decide	follow	parents	tired
code	easy	pants	red	voluntary

Sean goes to Jefferson Elementary School. Most of the

students follow the school dress _____. The colors are

_____1_____

_____ and brown. Sean wears a red shirt and brown

_____2_____

_____. Getting dressed is fast and _____.

____3____ ____4____

Students don't have to follow the dress code. It's _____.

____5____

Parents can decide if they want their children to _____

____6____

the dress code or not. Sean's _____ want him to

____7____

follow the dress code.

One of Sean's friends never follows the dress code. His

name is Keenan. Keenan wears funny T-shirts and old jeans. His

clothes are very _____.

____8____

Sean wants to dress like Keenan. He is _____

____9____

of red and brown. Sean wants his parents to _____

____10____

that he doesn't have to follow the dress code.

Write Some Reasons

What do some parents think about their children following a
dress code at school? Do they like the idea? Why or why not?
What do some children think about dress codes?

1. _Some parents think_ _____ .

2. _____ .

3. _____ .

4. _Some children think_ _____ .

5. _____ .

6. _____ .

Looking for School Clothes

Practice the dialog with a partner.

I think we need to buy you some
new school clothes.

**Why? What's wrong with what
I'm wearing?**

You need to wear a white shirt to school.

Is this T-shirt okay?

No, it isn't. You need a shirt with a collar.

I have a green and white shirt with a collar.

Sorry, it needs to be all white.

Then we need to go shopping. I don't have one.

On Sale

Read the ad for dress-code clothing for school.

School Uniform Sale at Kid Town!

Dress your child in comfortable, stylish school clothes that fit right and last a long time. Everything is machine washable.

Girls: Jumpers $16.99, Skirts $13.99, Pants $18.99, Polo shirts $11.99

Boys: Pants $18.99, Shorts $13.99, Polo shirts $11.99

Colors available in tops:
white, hunter green, navy blue, red, gold
Bottoms come in khaki, navy blue, hunter green, and black

Sizes: 8 to 20 regular, slim, and husky

Check our catalog or Web site for additional items.

Answer the questions.

1. What is the name of the store in this ad?

2. What is on sale?

3. How do you clean these clothes?

4. What item for girls costs $13.99?

5. How much are pants for boys?

6. Are boys' and girls' polo shirts the same price?

7. What sizes are available?

8. Do tops come in black?

9. Where can you look for other types of clothing?

Problem Solving

Your child complains and doesn't want to follow the school dress code. What can you do? Put a check next to the good ideas. Write other good ideas on the lines below.

_____ 1. I can explain why the dress code is a good idea.

_____ 2. I can find my child a school that doesn't have a dress code.

_____ 3. I can try to convince all parents to support the dress code.

_____ 4. I can punish my child for not following the dress code.

_____ 5. I can allow my child to sometimes wear something more colorful, stylish, or casual.

_____ 6. I can agree and tell my child the dress code isn't important.

_____ 7. I can call the school principal for advice.

✔ 8. I can _____.

✔ 9. I can _____.

Topics for Discussion or Writing

1. How can following the school dress code help a child? How can it help parents?

2. Do any schools in your community have a dress code or uniform? What do the students wear? What kind of clothing is not allowed?

1. Has your child ever been hurt at school? How?
2. What are some safety rules on the school playground?

Playground Safety

It's recess time, and Renata and Alice are playing outside on the playground. They are jumping rope. But it's very cold today, and Renata isn't wearing her jacket. She wants to go back to her classroom and put it on. She has to hurry. Recess is almost over. Renata starts to run back to her class.

Mrs. Russo is watching the students on the playground. She sees Renata running and says, "Walk, please! Running on the playground is against school rules. If you fall down, you can get hurt."

The blacktop on the playground is hard. Running is dangerous there. Renata remembers the rule and walks the rest of the way.

Renata goes inside and puts on her jacket. She looks at the clock. There are only five more minutes of recess. Her friend Alice is waiting for her. Renata forgets about Mrs. Russo's warning. She starts running, but then she slips and falls down. She scrapes her knee. It hurts a lot.

Mrs. Russo sees Renata sitting on the blacktop holding her knee. Renata is crying. "I'm sorry you fell down," Mrs. Russo says. "Remember, no running on the playground. It's dangerous. You need to go to the nurse's office. She'll put a bandage on your knee."

Answer the Questions

1. What are Renata and Alice doing at recess time?

2. How is the weather today?

3. Why does Renata want to go back to her classroom?

4. Why does Renata have to hurry?

5. Who is watching the students on the playground?

6. What does Mrs. Russo say is against school rules?

7. What does Renata forget?

8. What happens to Renata?

9. What does Renata need for her knee?

Check the Sentence That Means the Same

1. It's recess time, and Renata and Alice are playing outside.

_____ **a.** Renata and Alice are playing before school.

_____ **b.** Renata and Alice are playing during a break from class time.

2. It's very cold today, and Renata isn't wearing her jacket.

_____ **a.** Renata needs a jacket, but she isn't wearing one.

_____ **b.** It's too warm for a jacket today.

3. Running on the playground is against school rules.

_____ **a.** It's OK to run on the playground sometimes.

_____ **b.** It's not OK to run on the playground.

4. Renata forgets about Mrs. Russo's warning.

_____ **a.** Renata doesn't like Mrs. Russo.

_____ **b.** Renata doesn't remember what Mrs. Russo said.

5. You need a bandage for your knee.

_____ **a.** You need to put on your jacket.

_____ **b.** You need something to cover the scrape on your knee.

What Happened First?

Put these events in order.

____ Renata puts on her jacket.

_1_ Renata and Alice are jumping rope.

____ Renata is crying.

____ Mrs. Russo says, "You need to go to the nurse's office."

____ Renata wants to go back to her classroom for a jacket.

____ Renata slips and falls down.

____ Mrs. Russo says, "Walk, please."

Reporting an Injury

Practice the dialog with a partner.

Are you OK?

No, I hurt my elbow and my knee. Ouch!

What happened?

I was running, and then I slipped and fell.

Running is dangerous on the playground. The blacktop is hard!

I wasn't thinking. I was in a hurry.

Do you need to see the nurse?

Yes. I need bandages for these scrapes.

Stand up and I will help you inside.

Check the Body Parts

There are many body parts that children sometimes injure.
Put a check next to places where children are most often
injured. Write other places for injuries below.

____ eye	____ head	____ nose
____ neck	____ knee	____ leg
____ back	____ shoulder	____ elbow
____ arm	____ mouth	____ hand

_____   _____   _____

How Did These Children Get Hurt?

1.   **2.**   **3.**   **4.**

1. _____

2. _____

3. _____

4. _____

Answer the Questions

1. What does your child like to do at recess?

2. How long is recess?

3. What does your child wear to school when it's cold?

4. Who usually watches your child during recess?

5. Does your child's school have a blacktop playground?

6. Does your child like to run on the playground?

7. What is your child's favorite part of the playground?

8. Does your child's school have a grassy or sandy field?

9. What kind of warnings do children get on the playground?

10. Does your child ever get hurt at school? How?

11. Does your child sometimes come home from school wearing a bandage?

Topics for Discussion or Writing

1. Should children follow safety rules on the playground? Why or why not?

2. What is the playground at your child's school like? Is it a safe area for children to play? Why or why not?

3. What other injuries can happen to a knee besides a scrape? Which injuries are the most serious?

1. How often is your child absent from school?
2. What are some good reasons to be absent from school?

She's Always Absent

Chau is a fifth-grade student at Pacific Elementary School. Chau is a very healthy girl. She isn't sick very often. But Chau is absent from school a lot. Sometimes she stays home to help take care of her younger brother and sister. Sometimes she goes with her grandmother to the doctor. Chau speaks English very well. She translates for her grandmother and the doctor.

Chau usually misses one day of school a week. That adds up to many days during the school year. These absences are unexcused. That means she does not have an acceptable reason to be absent.

Chau doesn't learn everything the other children learn. She misses important lessons in class. She misses student activities and homework assignments. She is always confused when she returns to class.

Chau's teacher is very worried. Chau is a very intelligent girl. But she can't advance to the sixth grade if she is absent so much. She may need to repeat the fifth grade.

The principal is concerned too. She plans to visit Chau's parents at home. She will bring a translator and explain that Chau needs to be in school every day. Her education is very important.

Answer the Questions

1. What is the name of Chau's school?

2. Is Chau sick very often?

3. Who does Chau help take care of?

4. Where does Chau go with her grandmother?

5. What does Chau do for her grandmother?

6. How much school does Chau miss?

7. Why are her absences unexcused?

8. What does Chau miss in class?

9. What grade may Chau need to repeat?

10. Who does the principal plan to visit?

Check the Sentence That Means the Same

1. Chau is absent from school a lot.

    ____ **a.** Chau misses many days of school.

    ____ **b.** Chau misses only a few days of school.

2. Chau translates for her grandmother and the doctor.

    ____ **a.** Chau helps her grandmother walk to the doctor.

    ____ **b.** Chau helps her grandmother and the doctor understand each other.

3. These absences are unexcused.

    ____ **a.** She has an acceptable reason to be absent.

    ____ **b.** She does not have an acceptable reason to be absent.

4. She is always confused when she returns to class.

    ____ **a.** She doesn't know what the other students are doing.

    ____ **b.** She comes back with her homework assignments.

5. She may need to repeat the fifth grade.

    ____ **a.** She may need to be in the fifth grade again next year.

    ____ **b.** She may need to go back to the fourth grade.

Write Some Reasons

Write some reasons why children are absent from school.
Tell whether each reason is acceptable or not.

1. _A child has the flu._

    This is a good reason for a child to be absent.

2. _____

    _____

3. _____

    _____

Parents Discussing an Absence

Practice the dialog with a partner.

Our son has a fever this morning.

So he needs to miss school today.

Yes. Can you call the school office and report the absence?

Is that really important?

Yes, it's very important. If we don't call, the school will say it's an unexcused absence.

You're right. That isn't good.

My Son Is Absent

Read the note Nicholas's sister brings to the school office.

March 14

Please excuse my son, Nicholas Timmons, from school today. He will be absent. He has a stomachache and a fever. I am taking him to the doctor this afternoon. I don't know if he will be well enough to go to school tomorrow. Nicholas is a kindergarten student in Mr. Geoffrey's class.

Thank you,
Diane Timmons

Write the answers.

1. Who wrote this note? _____

2. Why will Nicholas be absent from school? _____

3. Can he go back to school tomorrow? _____

4. Where is Nicholas going in the afternoon? _____

5. What grade is Nicholas in? _____

6. Does Nicholas have an acceptable reason for being absent?

   _____

7. Who is Mr. Geoffrey? _____

8. How can you tell if your child has a fever? _____

   _____

Problem Solving

Your neighbor's child misses school a lot. You are worried about the child. What can you do? Put a check next to the good ideas. Write other good ideas on the lines below.

_____ **1.** I can tell the parents that education is important.

_____ **2.** I can forget about it. It's not my business.

_____ **3.** I can call the police.

_____ **4.** I can ask the child why he or she misses school.

_____ **5.** I can call the school principal for advice.

_____ **6.** I can offer to get the child's homework.

_____ **7.** I can ask the parents why the child misses school.

✓ **8.** I can _____.

✓ **9.** I can _____.

Topics for Discussion or Writing

1. When do some families need a child to help translate?

2. Why does a child sometimes need to repeat a grade in school?

3. What can you do if your child has to miss many days of school?

Answer Key

Lesson 1

Answer the Questions (p. 5)
1. almost every day
2. a bowl of cereal
3. cartoons
4. turn off the TV and go to school
5. He walks.
6. about 15 minutes
7. She marks Alain tardy.

Check the Sentence That Means the Same (p. 6)
1. a, 2. b, 3. a, 4. a, 5. a, 6. b

Late for School (p. 8)
1. He has a dentist appointment.
2. 8:30
3. He has a toothache.
4. by 10:00 or so
5. fourth
6. yes

Lesson 2

Answer the Questions (p. 11)
1. at his desk
2. third
3. math
4. His head itches.
5. to Mrs. Colwell's office
6. lice and nits
7. Ben's mother
8. when the lice and nits are all gone

Complete the Story (p. 12)
1. other
2. scratching
3. itches
4. nurse
5. hair
6. lice
7. immediately
8. shampoo
9. nits
10. completely

What Happened First? (p. 13) 6, 5, 2, 3, 7, 1, 4

A Letter to Parents (p. 14)
1. pediculosis
2. through contact or when children share brushes, combs, hats, and coats
3. the school
4. itching
5. tiny white eggs
6. with special shampoo, combs, and cleaning at home
7. so other children don't catch lice
8. the school nurse
9. yes

Lesson 3

Answer the Questions (p. 17)
1. Somalia
2. Arabic
3. yes
4. a long skirt, sandals, and a scarf
5. pants and dresses
6. no
7. no one
8. two girls in Naja's class
9. no
10. sorry for her

Which Category Is It? (p. 18)

Lunch Foods	Clothing	Countries
1. fruit	1. dress	1. China
2. rice	2. pants	2. Mexico
3. sandwiches	3. scarf	3. Somalia
4. vegetables	4. skirt	4. United States

Same Meaning (p. 18)
1. She eats alone.
2. Her native language is Arabic.
3. Naja is fluent in English.

What Are These Children Wearing? (p. 20)
1. long skirt, sandals, scarf
2. shorts, T-shirt, tennis shoes
3. dress, sweater, shoes
4. pants, shirt, shoes

Lesson 4

Answer the Questions (p. 23)
1. in the cafeteria
2. 12:00
3. very sad
4. four
5. they aren't very hungry or they don't like it
6. Vietnam
7. no
8. good food in garbage cans

Complete the Story (p. 24)
1. rules
2. push
3. down
4. container
5. sandwich
6. pocket
7. garbage
8. friends
9. wait
10. throw

What's for Lunch? (p. 26)
1. Thursday
2. Monday
3. juice or milk
4. cheese pizza, green salad, pudding, juice, milk
5. no
6. Thursday and Friday
7. Wednesday
8. pineapple

Lesson 5

Answer the Questions (p. 29)
1. Ana's mother
2. California
3. Ana's grandmother
4. a contract
5. her schoolwork
6. Ana, her mother, and Mr. Kennedy
7. the next week
8. she reads, writes, and does math
9. after one month
10. better

Which Category Is It? (p. 30)

Periods of Time	Schoolwork	States in the U.S.
1. day	1. assignment	1. California
2. month	2. lesson	2. Florida
3. week	3. project	3. New York
4. year	4. report	4. Texas

Matching (p. 30) 1. f, 2. b, 3. a, 4. g, 5. d, 6. c, 7. e

What Happened First? (p. 31) 6, 4, 2, 1, 7, 5, 3

Ana's Book Report (p. 32)
1. number 2
2. adventure story

3. Yes. The illustrator is listed.
4. Yes. She says, "and others."
5. She could tell what jungle it is, what city it is, etc.
6. No. She can describe one exciting part.
7. Yes. It's her favorite.

Lesson 6

Answer the Questions (p. 35)
1. on a field trip
2. by bus
3. four
4. stay with their group
5. elephants
6. sleeping
7. worried
8. They were more interesting.

Check the Sentence That Means the Same (p. 36)
1. a, 2. a, 3. b, 4. a, 5. a, 6. b

What Happened First? (p. 37) 4, 6, 1, 2, 7, 3, 5

Class Field Trip (p. 38)
1. no
2. $2.50 for bus transportation
3. a sack lunch
4. comfortable walking shoes, a hat, and sunscreen
5. 5
6. Answers may vary.
7. the permission slip at the bottom
8. say that it's OK

Lesson 7

Answer the Questions (p. 41)
1. a telephone bill, some ads, and a letter from school
2. three
3. how Sonya is doing in school
4. no
5. at a conference with the teacher
6. a translator
7. She doesn't want a neighbor to know what the teacher says about her daughter; a report card is personal.
8. no

Complete the Story (p. 42)
1. report
2. another
3. translator
4. questions
5. school
6. letters
7. explain
8. writes
9. daughter
10. know

Sonya's Report Card (p. 44)
1. reading and writing
2. no
3. writing stories and reading them aloud
4. math
5. encourage her to check her work
6. practicing math with her
7. yes

Lesson 8

Answer the Questions (p. 47)
1. 2:45 P.M.
2. The children leave their classrooms.
3. Some walk home, and some get on buses.
4. He stays at school.
5. until about 5:30 P.M.
6. They don't want him to be home alone.
7. no

8. Eli
9. He doesn't want to have too much homework to finish at home.
10. His father picks him up.

Check the Sentence That Means the Same (p. 48)
1. b, 2. a, 3. a, 4. b, 5. b, 6. a

After-School Program Rules (p. 50)
1. 3:00 P.M.
2. 6:00 P.M.
3. emergency contacts
4. The parents may be charged a late fee, and their child may be withdrawn from the program.
5. no
6. 15 hours
7. no

Lesson 9

Answer the Questions (p. 53)
1. straight to her bedroom
2. her crying
3. He knocks on her door and then opens it.
4. two
5. Inés's clothes
6. bad names
7. making it miserable
8. the principal
9. the rule that says you must treat other people with respect
10. no

Which Category Is It? (p. 54)

School Supplies	Emotions	Parts of a Room
1. backpack	1. angry	1. ceiling
2. lunchbox	2. depressed	2. door
3. notebook	3. furious	3. floor
4. pencils	4. miserable	4. window

Matching (p. 54) 1. d, 2. f, 3. g, 4. a, 5. b, 6. e, 7. c

What Happened First? (p. 55) 3, 5, 1, 6, 7, 2, 4

What Is Happening to These Students? (p. 56)
1. Students are calling her names.
2. Students are laughing at him.
3. Someone is kicking his backpack.
4. Someone is pushing her.

Lesson 10

Answer the Questions (p. 59)
1. to correct wrong answers on his multiplication test
2. no
3. He counts on his fingers or uses a pencil and paper.
4. his father
5. memorize the answers
6. multiplication flash cards
7. every evening
8. yes
9. He doesn't have any wrong answers to correct.

Complete the Story (p. 60)
1. wrong
2. answers
3. addition
4. remember
5. fingers
6. needs
7. flash cards
8. practice
9. assignment
10. doesn't

Parent-Teacher Conference (p. 62)

1. every week
2. 5
3. 50
4. She has a very hard time.
5. She feels nervous and starts guessing.
6. practice addition facts with her at home
7. that Alisha feel confident about solving problems

Lesson 11

Answer the Questions (p. 65)

1. She's always talking
2. behave in class
3. next to Albert
4. no
5. Justine is talking to Albert.
6. angry
7. listening
8. She says she is very sorry and she isn't going to talk anymore in class.
9. one more chance
10. at a table alone

Check the Sentence That Means the Same (p. 66)

1. a, 2. a, 3. a, 4. b, 5. b, 6. a

What Happened First? (p. 67) 3, 2, 5, 1, 4, 7, 6

Lesson 12

Answer the Questions (p. 71)

1. well
2. tomorrow
3. very excited
4. a big dog
5. uncomfortable
6. no
7. not going to other people's houses
8. home
9. at school
10. He doesn't want anything bad to happen to his son.

Which Category Is It? (p. 72)

Places to Live	Pets	Emotions
1. apartment	1. cat	1. disappointed
2. house	2. dog	2. excited
3. mobile home	3. fish	3. sorry
4. townhouse	4. turtle	4. uncomfortable

Same Meaning (p. 72)

1. John invites Shiro to come over to his house tomorrow.
2. He doesn't know where John lives.
3. I don't want to hurt John's feelings.

A Message from Mrs. Anderson (p. 74)

1. Kathleen Anderson
2. to invite Shiro over to play with John
3. He can ride the bus with John.
4. at work
5. Lisa, the babysitter
6. Mrs. Anderson will drive him.
7. 555-7410

Lesson 13

Answer the Questions (p. 77)

1. Lincoln Elementary School
2. They follow the dress code.
3. a white blouse and blue pants or a blue skirt
4. follow the dress code
5. Shannon
6. colorful and stylish
7. She is tired of them.
8. colorful and stylish, like Shannon's

Complete the Story (p. 78)

1. code
2. red
3. pants
4. easy
5. voluntary
6. follow
7. parents
8. casual
9. tired
10. decide

On Sale (p. 80)

1. Kid Town
2. school uniforms
3. in the washing machine
4. skirts
5. $18.99
6. yes
7. 8–20 regular, slim, and husky
8. no
9. Kid Town's catalog or web site

Lesson 14

Answer the Questions (p. 83)

1. jumping rope
2. very cold
3. to put on her jacket
4. Recess is almost over.
5. Mrs. Russo
6. running on the playground
7. Mrs. Russo's warning
8. She slips and falls down.
9. a bandage

Check the Sentence That Means the Same (p. 84)

1. b, 2. a, 3. b, 4. b, 5. b

What Happened First? (p. 85) 4, 1, 6, 7, 2, 5, 3

How Did These Children Get Hurt? (p. 86)

1. She fell on the blacktop.
2. He fell off the jungle gym.
3. The ball hit her in the face.
4. They ran into each other.

Lesson 15

Answer the Questions (p. 89)

1. Pacific Elementary School
2. no
3. her younger brother and sister
4. to the doctor
5. She translates.
6. usually one day a week
7. She does not have an acceptable reason to be absent.
8. important lessons, student activities, and homework assignments
9. fifth
10. Chau's parents

Check the Sentence That Means the Same (p. 90)

1. a, 2. b, 3. b, 4. a, 5. a

My Son Is Absent (p. 92)

1. Diane Timmons, Nicholas's mother
2. He has a stomach-ache and a fever.
3. His mother doesn't know.
4. to the doctor
5. kindergarten
6. yes
7. Nicholas's teacher